THE MAN AMONG
THE SEALS

&

INNER WEATHER

THE MAN AMONG
THE SEALS

&

INNER WEATHER

THE FIRST TWO BOOKS OF POEMS
BY

DENIS JOHNSON

CARNEGIE MELLON UNIVERSITY PRESS
PITTSBURGH 2017

Acknowledgments

Some of the poems in *The Man Among the Seals* were first published in *Cloud Marauder*, *Confluence*, *Intro II* (Bantam Books and McCall Publishers), *Iowa State Liquor Store*, *Kansas City Times*, *North American Review*, *Sou'wester*, *Suction*, and *Quickly Aging Here* (a Doubleday Anchor book).

Some of the poems in *Inner Weather* were first published in *American Poetry Review*, *Skywriting*, *The Iowa Review*, *Twelve Poems*, and *Intro: 6*.

The Man Among the Seals was published by Stonewall Press in 1969; *Inner Weather* was published by Graywolf Press in 1976.

Cover design: Bronwyn Kuehler

First Carnegie Mellon University Press Edition, October 2017

Library of Congress Control Number: 2017937497
ISBN: 978-0-88748-627-2

10 9 8 7 6 5 4 3 2

CONTENTS

The Man Among the Seals

Inner Weather

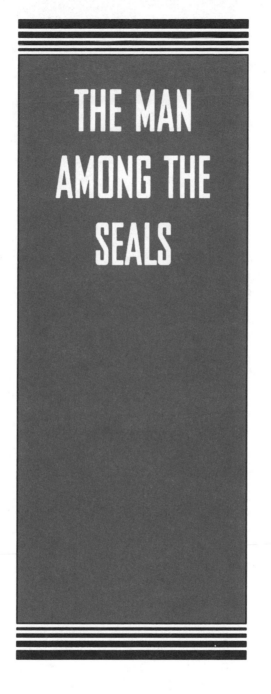

THE MAN AMONG THE SEALS

"Did you have rapport with the seals?" the judge asked. "I guess I did have rapport with the seals," Giordano said. Despite the rapport, Basel fined Giordano $50 for annoying the seals.

—AP *Wire Service*

Quickly Aging Here

I

nothing to drink in
the refrigerator but juice from
the pickles come back
long dead, or thin
catsup. i feel i am old

now, though surely i
am young enough? i feel that i have had
winters, too many heaped cold

and dry as reptiles into my slack skin.
i am not the kind to win
and win.
no i am not that kind, i can hear

my wife yelling, "goddamnit, quit
running over," talking to
the stove, yelling, "i
mean it, just stop," and i am old and

2

i wonder about everything: birds
clamber south, your car
kaputs in a blazing, dusty
nowhere, things *happen,* and constantly you

wish for your slight home, for

your wife's rusted
voice slamming around the kitchen. so few

of us wonder why
we crowded, as strange,
monstrous bodies, blindly into one
another till the bed

choked, and our range
of impossible maneuvers was gone,
but isn't it because by dissolving like so
much dust into the sheets we are crowding

south, into the kitchen, into
nowhere?

Boy Aged Six Remembering

this has been a
busy day. in the morning there was
his mother, calling to him
from the garden and he ran
thinking that he was

a tower into the light around her.
he had wanted to
bring her water, or a
small thing. later

he will perhaps harness the afternoon
and send it ahead to pull
us down, or up, who can
say for later?

now is the thing, now
with the light around the house
in the yard and earlier,
before lunch, when he saw his father

at the well sending the pail
far down into the cooler, hidden
water; earlier, when he saw
his father reaching down like

that into the water, and did not
recognize the composition of a
memory, or how they, these people, are
often composed of memories.

Victory

the woman whose face has just finished breaking
with a joy so infinite

and heavy that it might be grief has won
a car on a giveaway show, for her family,

for an expanse of souls that washes from a million
picture tubes onto the blank reaches

of the air. meanwhile, the screams are packing
the air to a hardness: in the studio

the audience will no longer move, will be caught
slowly, like ancient, staring mammals, figuring

out the double-cross within the terrible progress
of a glacier. here, i am suddenly towering

with loneliness, repeating to this woman's
only face, *this time, again, i have not won.*

Spring

by now even the ground
deep under the ground has dried.
the grass becoming green

does not quite remember the last year,
or the year before, or the centuries
that kept passing over. all of these blades thought
that america's grief over the ruptured

flesh of its leaders
was another wind going into the sky.
a rabbit stiffens

with hard sorrow up from the grass
and runs. well,
it is another spring and in the clouds

it is the ranging spectacle of a crowd
of congressmen accusing one another, each
moving in his own shadow against the next.

Why I Might Go to the Next Football Game

sometimes you know
things: once at a
birthday party a little

girl looked at her new party
gloves and said she
liked me, making suddenly the light much
brighter so that the very small

hairs shone above her lip. i felt
stuffed, like a swimming pool, with
words, like i knew something that was in
a great tangled knot. and when we sat

down i saw there were
tiny glistenings on her
legs, too. i knew
something for sure then. but it

was too big, or like the outside too
everywhere, or maybe
hiding inside, behind
the bicycles where i later

kissed her, not using my tongue. it was
too giant and thin to squirm
into, and be so well inside of, or
too well hidden to punch, and feel. a few

days later on the asphalt playground i
tackled her. she skinned her

elbow, and i even
punched her and felt her, felt

how soft the hairs were. i thought
that i would make a fine football-playing
poet, but now i know
it is better to be an old, breathing

man wrapped in a great coat in the stands, who
remains standing after each play, who knows
something, who rotates in his place
rasping over and over the thing

he knows: "whydidnhe *pass*? the other
end was wide *open*! the end
was wide *open*! the end was wide *open* . . ."

A Woman Is Walking Alone Late at Night

no one can know through what silence she moves. for long
nights, through an eternity of stealth
she has tracked her own dim form drifting there
ahead, has seen her
self, lost again, keep swimming through this wealth
of solitude. it must be wrong,

that i should watch her. i'm afraid that she
will turn her eyes to me, show me the fast
outdistancing of years she sees, and i
would clutch terribly
after my past days as if for the last
thing i would see, as if for me
all those long moments, each friendly second i'd known
was lost, gone to the air, was really gone.

The Dry Dry Land. Here

the dry dry land. here
and there from the
rasp and muscle of its flatness
a tree gushes forth. i

have seen trees, have
heard them at night being
dragged into the sky.
i know that they are very
real. i know they know.

lover, i am not
a tree, you would
never mistake me
for one, my arid movements

for its flowing coolness. but
sometimes in the dark silken
air of this room

i feel that we are
a liquid jumble of trees
falling interminably away from
the land, its dry infinitude.

The Glimpsed Old Woman in the Supermarket

from the sidewalk i can see her,
as she barely stands, easily mired
among supermarket products,
as if rapidly and all
too soon the swimming hole
had turned solid. around her,

housewives search for a detergent
that will cleanse away the years;
locking her vision into
a box of tide she must see
the finances crumbling
in the distant bank, or the remembered
friends, who she knew
would be winding up here.

i cannot touch
you. i would like to hold you forth
and say, here is the television
sign-off music; this
is the vision crept up on
by cloudiness, first in the corners;
here is the morning

trickling from the house. but i can't
reach you: just as easily the sidewalk
holds me, and i love you,
i want to crook my finger beneath
your dress, and unearth
your trembling, delicate loins.

Poem Questioning the Existence of the Sea

in exactly the same
way that the animals were launched
onto the sand, frightened

after so many eons by the sudden
darkness of the sea,
a very large number

of children plunge daily in their last great
evolutionary spasm from the wombs
of pale, inarticulate women. it is wide

and kind of empty where one stands,
now, years after, and floats
drastically his hips

against the pin-ball machine. outside,
the detective wail of his own
impossible child is overturning the streets,

as he maneuvers this unloveable machine, deftly
and like a great ship,
through the stages of his life. just

as confused as ever, i observe
the buildings increasing under the sky,
knowing that soon i must

become him, and elude
my children and bludgeon the waves
in skillful drunkenness. i tremble,

like an old indian, for just a little
rain over this desert.

Telling the Hour

if you want to know
the time you must look
at a clock, or stare continuously
into the moon,

until it grows round like a clock.
under the moon growing round
a hunter strolls; he must be saying,

"i have killed an animal." however,
as the evening draws
close in for a better look, it is

nine p.m. and the hunter's arms
are loaded with air, his belly
swells with the solitude. he is saying,
"i *think* i have killed an animal,

a barely visible bird,
at eight p.m., or the dim
figure of a woman bent over
her sewing, in a distant house,

who glanced occasionally
at the big moon. and i shot
a telephone pole as it strained
into the sky, wanting desperately the moon."

as he continues among the trees,
the ticking of the city becomes
larger, moving the birds and insects

from the air, rattling

the moon so that it opens
and tolls down upon the hunter.
his hands try to caress the sudden,
awkward hush, and he wonders more often,
"have i killed an animal?"

Retirement

i would like to be just an old man with my gin,
retiring even from these leaves into
my big, gradual silence beyond the wood
and it will be good,
wife, because i have pointed to you,
and you have become real. within

this darker stillness my eyes grow too wide.
it must be that seeing you in the trees
becoming softer than i ever dreamed
has made it all seem
a multitude of nonsense, all the seas,
the planets, all i wrote. i lied,

i swear to you i lied, becoming old and so
very drunk, when i did not lie to you.

The Year's First Snow

emptying into
the freezing, quiet alleys

there is the voice of a single
ferreting drunk. if he is singing

it is lovely, and if he talks on
strangely, he, at least,

understands. by the river, noiselessly,
some lovers have frozen

in the winter, and they will be taken
away, with the floods of spring.

in an upper window
of the county jail, the sleepless man

who was framed knows
that all along, all along,

this snow that rests
more heavily over the reach of branches

has been descending.

On a Busy Street a Man Walks Behind a Woman

there is the chance that you will step
ahead of me into the traffic
alive, and that there will be
an accident. always i am walking,

i am seeing your heels and thinking
of something else, but always i am
asking you to remember: if you step carefully

into the screeching
of tires and become bloody, i must not
be the one extending himself awkwardly

into the confusion to say, my dear
mrs. hutchins, do
forgive the way we have arranged

your body, dead like that
on the pavement, but surely you
understand? it must
not be me who is the one

fisherman to fish you up drowned among
all that seaweed. it cannot
be me looking in all
directions for help, knowing all

along that it is just you
and me, finally, and that i am
alone to hear the sound of the breakfast
bell opening as it did

into the corners of the barnyard, and your
mother's voice calling back
and forth among the animals. am i

positioned here alone to welcome
you from such a very distant
place, and must i now tell you what every

second in your life, what all the
breathing and the continual inching
forward of the body through each and every
day, when i am so absolutely

young, when i am so
unprepared, must i
tell you what it has all
at last come to? you are

dead, mrs. hutchins, amid this
mob craning to see your own blood,
which has somehow

gotten away from you in all
the excitement—i am so truly sorry,
of course it isn't fair, you weren't
prepared, but don't you see it works

this way for all of us, for instance that
i am here just isn't fair, either, because
of my unpreparedness, because of my lack

of anything to say except you're dead,
you're dead, i didn't
do it, i didn't do it.

Checking the Traps

morning,
the door opening, changing
into a doorway. half

the night i stayed awake and smoked
and watched the mousetraps.
the mice were there, nudging
into cups and plates, one fell

into the toaster, but escaped.
they waited until i gave up and slept to die.
for these mice
the night will be long. i heard

the iron snapping
in my sleep and dreamed my wife was
closing the door.

two mice are dead, for my wife.
mice make her legs
go watery, as they do sometimes after her climax.

one mouse's head is barely
in the trap, one eye probing
toward the ceiling where i could tell him
there is nothing.
the other mouse is flung willingly under the iron

bar. i wonder, were they
married? was she pregnant? they are
going out together,

in the garbage this morning. it was
morning when we were married.
it has been morning

for a long time. that mouse, with his
eye. did he hear the iron snapping,
and dream it was his

wife with her stretching, laden tits
closing the door?

The Man Among the Seals

for Ed Schroeder

at night here in the park it is different:

the man by the seal pool stalks
through an acute emptiness, encircled
by the city. is he
taking off his clothes?

by day i have seen
the seals, enclosed, blundering
among the spattered rocks. they climb
like prisoners of a ferris wheel, above
their pool and above
the peanuts floating through
air, high over the sudden, too large

teeth of the spectators. but at night
without their land-locked captors moving
gracefully by, the seals
seem less inept, even

on the hostile rocks.
before dawn they rise
and dive, becoming masters
in the water. the figure in

underwear on the left is not
a seal. before me and
an audience of trees he has
joined the seals. drunk, perhaps,

and, a staggerer on land,
perhaps he hopes to move cleanly,
like a seal, through water. or,

sober, perhaps he dives to assume
the clumsiness now shed by the seals: then
he will tumble drunk onto
the ground, and the seals, plunging

landward, will find
no awkwardness among the rocks, will
no longer wonder deep
within themselves at a dry hardness
which is not ice. each day

he will return, wetness
forever staining through his pants,
to watch his seals as they rise
above the rocks to pluck the floating

bits of food, as they slide through
the air over the trees, the
ferris wheel grown

stationary with shame, the tiny
unfamiliar bodies jerking
under balloons through the lighted park.

Crossing Over the Ice

i should have brought
an axe to this white place and seen
for sure if, far beneath,
a city is falling irretrievably away.
as it is i can only guess

that this spot, warmer
than the rest, is where the tallest
steeple was cut loose to unmoor the town.
i wonder: could i nudge my vision

over onto the spaces below?
it has thus far been
easy to locate myself, somewhere between hands
warming in pockets and the hands that waken,
empty, out of the shadows
of buildings. i know

what's going on; the stars
evade the oceans, thank goodness,
and just here there are
the trees fumbling with roots under the earth.
to chip through to a town

that will not come back might
put me anywhere, i might become
that someone on the farther bank, who is standing

still within the movement of trees, as if
one step would lose him gradually
into the stars. he may be

the one who has leaned
his head into the air underneath and seen
another dawn glowing like a deep fish,
seen, as here above,

the citizens in the morning
growing tinier, weightless
and lost from their families,
preparing for beautiful
supermarkets, for an endlessness
of downward flight under an expanse of snow.

Upon Waking

at the far edge of earth, night
is going away. another
poem begins. slumped over

the typewriter i must get this
exactly, i want to make it
clear this morning that your

face, as it opens
from its shadow, is more
perfect than yesterday; and

that the light, as it
hesitates over the approach
of your smile, has given this

aching bed more than warmth,
more than poems; someway

a generous rose, or a very
delicate arrangement of sounds,
has come to peace in this new room.

A Child Is Born in the Midwest

as i look on your struggle i remember
i have seen arriving from movie theaters
the forms of people
disgraced, slanting heavily out of the cold,
their coats, the muscles under the skin
fraying, given up to the air.
and later, near morning,
i have seen their figures compelled
from the panic and emptiness of the town asleep
into all-night diners, which flounder, exhausted.
outside the towns the wide plains
are delirious
with frozen animals,
and the sky is rising with moons and moons.
these faces lifted over the street

are not moons. even so, they are
lost somewhere between worlds and home,
in a town that can't quite hold onto the earth.
i listen to your tiny,
unbelieving anguish,
and i wonder if i have known
these faces in another time;
and i think that you have come here, drifting
through universes of cold
because no longer, no longer
could the womb contain your loneliness.

To Enter Again

for the astronauts on the occasion
of their re-entry

for the first few instants in
this jungled machine we were all
at once human. then
we became confused monsters,
and then we were, as before,

sardines waiting to land hung
over like sardines.
for the first few instants
we had been dragged
outside of everything. but

the cracks began to show, each
of us was too much the
other, and we were once

again inside our terribly good
balloon, revolving and knowing
far too much.

the first day we slept
little, we examined and counted
the stars. we thought we should. and now
we sleep most of the time, dreaming

ourselves away from this haze
of tubes and gauges. we have learned: we
have been brought here to

wait, and to learn

to live packed
in forever, waiting to be pried
out. to live here truly
washed by the sea, turning end
over end, waiting to halt,

and breathe, but never
halting. waiting to slide at
last toward the freshly lighted

earth, there to wait and dive again far
down into tubes and fantasies.
the moon lies
there beyond us, cringing toward the neat

package of stars, not
waiting. below, in dreams, the earth scatters
in all directions way from
itself, and yearns
toward us, toward our distant perfection.

Drunk in the Depot

for Bob Zimmerman

drunk here in the railway depot
i can recall your train budging
forward in that other depot, that first
squash of steam making
your window real and solid. that is

why i am jumping down onto
the tracks, or because i am a gazelle.
i left later, by bus, and now
the city is gray and vacant, so i

am bounding out of the depot along
the tracks though i think
i am here to see someone
off. the train moved and you were

windowed in and everything was
final. or i might have left
by plane from the airport. no,

it was bus. i am supposed to
wave goodbye to a girl. that
was the last time i

saw you, so i will keep
moving down the tracks because
i *am* some kind of zebra, because
these railway tracks are mashing
like ridiculous snowshoes into

the distance. she thinks i am

cute, in a grubby, nonsexual
way. it was summer then; now
it is winter, with all
the roads stationed outside

the houses and the snow coming
to get them. it should have been
night, and it is.

The Cabinet Member

. . . *wake up in the morning:*
a critical editorial, or a Herb Block cartoon.
RICHARD NIXON

wake up
in the morning: a critical
editorial, or a herb block
cartoon. sometimes, if my wife

would just leave me alone things
would be all right. you should see
this cartoon,
or the poor sogginess
of this bacon, you don't believe this

country's going down
and not up. the sewers
demand attention. the potomac

is swallowing up all the love,
and society is
killing itself, for love. if i

had a dog there would be
more love in it for me. if
i had something in my hands.

In a Rented Room

this is a good dream, even if the falling is
no less real, and even if my feet will crumble

on the lurking ground. my throat itches, and i am
awake in this room which is no less vacant for

all my presence and there are no aspirin. here
is the sun with its tired surprise, the morning. there

are the cars and streets moving in the usual
fashion. the room wants to be rid of me. it must

fall open and communicate with other dim,
stifled rooms when i have slaughtered my body in

the sheets and fumbled streetward to sooth the itch. what
do you learn, room? what have you told, why are the stains

and the accusing glasses pointing so when i
return? there was the girl some time ago. *she* would

want to know where the guilt comes from, that hums over
the bed and descends, like an uncaring thumb, to

blot me out. she would help me, when the universe
has fooled me again, and the joke has gone too far,

when the itch, climbing, deep, remains after bottle
after bottle, and i inch toward death and i

must poke my body into a thousand vacant
darknesses before i strike the correct sleep, and dream.

Driving Toward Winter

miraculously,
there is the sun, coming back.
beneath it the cows wander, more
exhausted, baffled by the sparseness
of the winter grass. were i
a cow staggering over vanishing grass,

i would feel like the man
in the story, the one where
he leaps into his sports car to find
that everything has become an ocean, saying
certainly i did not expect
the sea. yesterday the numerous
actual cars spilled over
solid hills. kissing

my wife i never wished for the sea. in
an agony of exactness, bent
into the tiny measuring dials i did not
yearn for these impossible waves,
or for the stopped movement
of trees. the wrecked,
liquid countryside unfolds
beyond me, and i am the last bubble of air,
searching for air.

licking bare dirt, the nearest cow
raises his head to me, not understanding.
i would tell him about the sun, how it
rolls nearer, hauling the spring.

but he peers at me as if through mist, as i
would peer through the fogged, cracking windows
of my fast car at the half-
distinguished movements of an unusual fish.

A Poem about Baseballs

for years the scenes bustled
through him as he dreamed he was
alive. then he felt real, and slammed

awake in the wet sheets screaming
too fast, everything moves
too fast, and the edges of things
are gone. four blocks away

a baseball was a dot against
the sky, and he thought, my
glove is too big, i will

drop the ball and it will be
a home run. *the snow falls*
too fast from the clouds,
and night is dropped and

snatched back like a huge
joke. is that the ball, or is
it just a bird, and the ball is
somewhere else, and i will
miss it? *and the edges are gone, my*

hands melt into the walls, my
hands do not end where the wall
begins. should i move
forward, or back, or will the ball

come right to me? i know i will
miss, because i always miss when it

takes so long. *the wall has no*
surface, no edge, the wall

fades into the air and the air is
my hand, and i am the wall. my
arm is the syringe and thus i

become the nurse, i am you,
nurse. if he gets
around the bases before the
ball comes down, is it a home

run, even if i catch it? *if we could*
slow down, and stop, we
would be one fused mass careening
at too great a speed through
the emptiness. if i catch

the ball, our side will
be up, and i will have to bat,
and i might strike out.

The Woman at the Slot Machine

if the children were not locked
into georgia, and texas, if

the husband were not packed away
cold, never to be fished

from air, the plunging down
of the handle might be less desperate

but alone now before
this last enemy, she juggles

for any victory. the jerked
handle offers a possible coming home. each

symbol come to rest clicks into
her eyes, because

it *is* there to be had, it
was there once, the old miracle come back

alive, when the bell
sang like a beautiful daughter and it was

harry, upstairs with his broken
leg, ringing for her, yelling, martha come hear

the radio, it's jack benny and he's playing
the violin.

The Mourning in the Hallway

my neighbor's voice occurs within the hall, sadly:
come back inside the house awhile before
you go away. his daughter does not hear
his oldest voice swear
that he will balance forward from that door
forever toward the spaces she

has left. and even i have felt this thing,
this leaning into the ocean like wild,
like aching beasts. my wife was not alone
when, deep in her bone
and tumbling eternally, our child
continued drowning. now, hearing

this man's face change against the tide his girl has gone
away with, i leap to hold my own son.

Out There Where the Morning

out there where the morning
is, the automobiles and citizens
are clattering along just
like pieces of the universe. from

my place by the window i can
examine an airplane as it crawls
from speck to speck on the glass.
i know that it is with
the same arrogant mechanical

lust that the pipes of the kitchen sink
are dissolving. i am
ready to believe that everything else is,
too. for instance this
room i am sure is
atom by atom taking leave. but here in

the disappearing room i am not too
heavily alone. printed on the
label of this cookie can is
the one assurance:

each cookie contains a joke.

and i know that this
is somehow good. i can
call my mother and say, mother
it is not what is true, but what

is good that now matters. mother,
mother, even here in this tumbling
jar of selves,
each cookie contains a joke,

each of us offers himself up whole
to some nearly invisible,
tasteless affirmation.
such sensation as we derive is derived

only from the joke. mother,
i am this morning electric. i am spinning
into the staccato punch line,
the end and the crumbling. i will

hear the laughter as it breaks up
and dissolves farther out in space,
as it grinds and echoes against the metal.

In Praise of Distances

as the winter slips up under
the palms of my hands, it is getting
harder to be a poet: i am woe
itself. my car fades

without pain from the parking lot. it
crumples to one knee, like
an elephant, startled
into lifelessness by the hungry bullets of winter.
the graveyard wavers
distantly. the car will no longer stand

between me and the debts nuzzling
at my door. i will no longer go rattling
among the miles as if

distance were a safe thing, as if i slammed
the ancient car door
in the face of all the noises.
my wife tells me, why don't you get
a job? but once i had a dog,

whose vital organs became
confused beneath his skin, until he died;
i will not leave this animal kingdom

until he comes back from the trees.
i will keep my nostrils
opened for the lonely jangle
of his collar landing over the buildings

or for some sign that he will be returning.
my hands will not
be filled with advertisements; so

they will be filled with the difficulty
that is winter. if he is lost,
farmers hoping for spring will discover
his voice among the corn stalks,

seeking a safe place to lie
quietly down. as i wait for him
by the window,
i have the suspicion that the meaning of things
will never be sorted out.

A Consequence of Gravity

my wife's voice yelling from
the window holds the distant echoes
of a thousand mothers-in-law, all the women,
all the weight, increasing, of this planet.

i will not listen. here in the yard i am watching
an old story: a child has dived
into the earth attempting to fly, and injured

farther than the skin he gives
his long syllable toward the moon.
there is no one to tell him he will settle

for years, in a gradual re-enactment
of this flight, against the earth,
as he cries over his miserable attachment
to the ground and mourns

that first unlucky generation
of airplanes, the lost inventions still burrowing
somewhere desperately away from the air,
making caves, making

no sense at all crushed into the sides of mountains.
i grow, like an imprisoned pilot,
heavier, near death, my face
makes mistakes in the last oxygen of the cockpit.

through the dusk the moon has rolled
again out into her private ocean. i cannot
help it, like a blank virgin she has retired

beyond the air, and here, bereft, surrounded
by grotesque, inedible women and the painful
breaking of another spring i admit it,
i will never touch her, hold her.

For the Death of the Old Woman

one after another along
the perspective of the street, the people
remain upright. my hands

are blacking out, from the cold,
dry body of this old woman.
she has died,

while she was sitting, concerned
somewhere in her house. growing
more beautiful, something has left

the big rocker, has moved
through the leaves brushing her window,
beyond the trees and first

national bank to a point
overlooking the collapse of cities.
the rivers are backing up

with whales
and wreckage, with
the crowds of foam becoming huge and

hanging to the factories that lean
over the wettening banks.
the figures

of graves diminish toward
the horizon:
on the street,

these faces are not chipped with grief,
as they leap after busses.
in the window of a store front a man

who did not know her adjusts
the limbs of a mannequin, and
the ascending voice

of a child wants to know, do the rivers freeze
by themselves, can you walk on them.

The Man Who Was Killed

whatever the wind says that divides
the surface of the river

into tiny, upward gestures of surprise
is not known, not here

by me on the bank. i have wondered
this same thing about the wintry faces of pedestrians,

i have wondered how much of this
is crazy and how much is real. he must have been

hearing the wind, to be so deeply
startled when the bullet rushed

from the assassin's control. he remembers always
how it was, to breathe. his eye

drifts through the streets in the city,
through the rain, dreaming after his life.

April 20, 1969

when i think that i am watching
the evening lengthen toward the end of this country,
i know there can be no sea
at the end of the pier. even
the sea has gone to hide deep
in the spaces below the sea, and the few
children who have stayed this long in the yard
are disappearing toward their dinners.

INNER
WEATHER

An Evening with the Evening

The night is very tall
coming down the street. The light
of the streetlights coming on
in sequence just in front of the dark,
this light is a prison
broken loose from itself.
The city has an expression
on its face like that of someone hoping

he will not be noticed,
it is like that of the man now watching
the processional flaring of the lamps from the corner,
beneath the bank sign.
He notices the city, he notices
the reflection of his own face in the city,
he wonders what the city must have done

to the night,
that it should avert itself like a debtor
while welcoming the night
with such display, such grim pomp, so courteous
a removal, before
the arrival of darkness,
of any competing darknesses that may have
managed to precede it there.

Suddenly it is the total blackness
with the numerous small lights of the face
of the city shining through it;
then it is the end,

which is only himself, going
home to his wife and children,
turning and trying to walk away from the darkness
that precedes him, darkness of which he is the center.

Winter

On the streets, which have gutters,
in the shadows of doorways, at
busstops, at this moment
and yesterday, before the bars, their breath
excluded in great
clouds, turning from the wind
to spit
and laugh horribly

at the life standing up inside them
with such pain as
loneliness permits, and the weather,
turning to each other
with jokes and lies, with the baggage
and garbage of their humanness as if one
they held it toward would
take it and thank them

is us, all of us, all dragged by the legs upstream
like poor stooges sunk to drowning
for a living.
On Clinton St. the bars explode
with the salt smell of us like the sea, and the tide
of rock and roll music, live
humans floating on it
out over the crimes of the night. How

unlike such outwardness the clenching back
of a man into himself is,
several of us are our own fists
There! emphasizing on the tabletop.

Prayer: That We May Be Given This Day the Usual Business

Some days the automobiles are smiling,
other days they
are morose;
and so it is with humans, always
going around crying, until one
day one of them is all smiles,
introducing, buying drinks.
Had you never met one,
these nevertheless would be known
to you readily by their descriptions,
these humans, heads, legs
and arms inexplicable, graduating
immaculately like the small
blossoms into this faith,
that soon, soon the moon
shall descend to touch
us each deeply,
here.
        But there is a shadow
        to touch each roof
        at six-thirty in
        this country, and it comes to them
        singly, this shadow, it falls down to each
        as he opens the door of his car,
        it wholly becomes the space
        behind each door, beneath each lid, top and cover
        he has closed, and turns from now.
        The instant he ceases smiling
        at his victims and beneficiaries and closes

his mouth he is filled so with blackness
it spills behind him even
in the broad noon.
Yet as he fumbles for correct change only, and is angry,
observes the long-stemmed roses
opening in the greenhouses
in the winter, and is afraid,
you find that you love him:
see how he polishes his car
though it holds the whisper of his death, be filled
with joy as he expends
himself like a breath
into this, the loveliest of air,
climbing into that instrument that goes quietly,
driven by bright fire.

The Two

The airplane is like silver
that bears the two of them
to Mexico under the sun

to be divorced. Disembarking
they begin to bicker
over small matters: She

wants to be divorced
in the morning, refreshed,
but he says forget all about

the morning, I want to do it now.
You cheap, continually drowning me,
she says, by God

I want a divorce. He says fine,
you've got it: right now.
She replies she would like to wait

till morning. This goes on.
The two work their hatred
till it is like a star reduced

to the dimensions of a jewel.
The airport is quiet. The janitor's
broom whispers to the floor,

the day talks to the night,
saying just what the ocean says
to the land, what the blood

is saying to the heart,
contained, but coming, going.

Looking Out the Window Poem

The sounds of traffic
die over the back lawn
to occur again in the low
distance.

The voices, risen, of
the neighborhood cannot
maintain that pitch
and fail briefly, start
up again.

Similarly my breathing rises
and falls while I look out
the window of apartment
number three in this slum,
hoping for rage, or sorrow.

They don't come to me
anymore. How can I lament
anything? It is all
so proper, so much
as it should be, now

the nearing cumulus
clouds, ominous,
shift, they are like the
curtains, billowy,
veering at the apex
of their intrusion on the room.
If I am alive now,
it is only

to be in all this
making all possible.
I am glad to be
finally a part
of such machinery. I was
after all not so fond
of living, and there comes
into me, when I see
how little I liked
being a man, a great joy.

Look out our astounding
clear windows before evening.
It is almost as if
the world were blue
with some lubricant,
it shines so.

There Are Trains Which Will Not Be Missed

They tell you if you write great poems
you will be lifted into the clouds
like a leaf which did not know

this was possible, you will never
hear of your darkness
again, it will become
distant while you become
holy, look,

they say, at the emptiness
of train tracks and it is poetry
growing up like flowers between
the ties, but those

who say this
are not in control of themselves
or of anything and they must

lie to you in order
that they may at night not bear witness
to such great distances cascading and such

eternities unwinding
around them as to cause even the most powerful
of beds to become silences, it

is death which continues
over these chasms and these
distances deliberately like a train.

Commuting

We understand well that we must hold
our lives up in our arms like the victims
of solitary, terrible accidents,
that we must still hold our lives to their promises

and hold ourselves up to our lives
to be sure always they are larger,
wholer, realer than we ourselves, though we
must carry them.
We on this train with our lives in our laps

are waiting patiently for the next moment
and maybe we will be lifted away by our lives
as are the moments we rise up to hold with us,
or maybe we will just slacken
above our drinks in the club car chatting baseball,
all of us headed
to apply for the same job, all of us qualified,

all of us turning now into snowflakes
too delicate,
yet each holding in itself a tiny
stark particle of darkness
and weight, the heart's cinder
turning over.

Employment in the Small Bookstore

The dust almost motionless
in this narrowness, this stillness,
yet how unlike a coffin
it is, sometimes letting a live one in,
sometimes out
                    and the air,
though paused, impends not a thing,
the silence isn't sinister,
and in fact not much goes on
at the Ariel Book Shop today,
no one weeps in the back
room full of books, old books, no one
is tearing the books to shreds, in fact
I am merely sitting here
talking to no one, no one being here,
and I am blameless.
                    More,
I am grateful for the job,
I am fond of the books and touch them,
I am grateful that King St. goes down
to the river, and that the rain
is lovely, the afternoon green.
If the soft falling away of the afternoon
is all there is, it is nearly
enough, just
                    let me hear the beautiful clear voice
of a woman in song passing
toward silence, and then
that will be all for me
at five o'clock.
                    I will walk

down to see the untended
sailing yachts of the Potomac
bobbing hopelessly in another silence,
the small silence that gets to be a long
one when the past stops talking
to you because it is dead,
                              and still you listen,
hearing just the tiny
agonies of old boats
on a cloudy day, in cloudy water.
Talk to it. Men are talking to it
by Cape Charles, for them it's the same
silence with fishing lines in their hands.
We are all looking at the river bearing the wreckage
so far away. We wonder how
the river ever came to be so
gray, and think that once there were
some very big doings on this river,
and now that is all over.

Working Outside at Night

The moon swells
and its yellow darkens
nearer the horizon
and soon all
the aluminum rooftops

shall appear, orange
and distinct beside
the orange sun,
while the diamond
flares in its vacuum

within. It is simple
to be with the shovel,
thoughtless, inhabited
by this divorce,
it is good

the luminous
machinery, silenced,
waits, nice
that the conveyor
belts choked with sand

convey nothing.
When I return home to
coffee at
7:45 the lithe
young girls will be going
to high school, pulling

to their mouths stark
cigarettes through
Arizona's sunlight.
These last few months
have been awful, and when

around five the roosters
alone on neighboring
small farms begin
to scream like humans
my heart just lies down,
a stone.

An Inner Weather

This is the middle of the night.
There are no stars. It's been lightly snowing
a while, and it is silent. Many men are sleepless,
and for some, within, it is blazing noon.
The commander cries in the street dirt,
the apprentice rides on the mayor.
And yet one pool of light
is succeeded by another tonight,
as always, amid silence, beneath the lamps,
but even these impenetrable things
waver, and aren't quite real,
and we take no comfort from them.
For the fathers parade as leering women,
the entrails of pets drape the sewer-grates.
Our shadows are black stumps.
Some of us fire
with our mouths open,
amazed, firing.
The cup is overturned by the dagger
and blood dots the window-glass.
This is the way of it
for many men this quiet night of snow.
The snow descends in a sparkling light but many are blind,
walking out without jackets as if into the sun,
and they would not say anything of the snow,
but would say only this
of the weather, that something falling burns on them.

The Supermarkets of Los Angeles

The supermarkets
of Los Angeles are blinding,
they are never closed,

they are defended
by the mountains
on the North, on

the Southeast by the
desert and on
the West by the large,

sad Pacific Ocean.

• • •

We enter such
brilliance as we entered
the world, without

shopping list, perfectly.
It is unpleasant,
but each is thinking

he may be here
to escape still worse.
What? There is nothing

out there other
than late winter,
Hollywood, the moments

before morning.

• • •

We are never alone
here: above our heads, though
close enough nearly

to touch, is television,
in which may be disclosed
our own faces. They do not

become us. They are
the little faces we wore
as children, now wrinkled,

as if we were not grown
but only aged. We want
to cleanse those wrinkles

of accumulate filth,
these faces whose names
are being withheld, so tiny

in the relaxed fist of
Los Angeles, hearing
Los Angeles singing

to the murdered. We see
the eyes, and we see
what the eyes see,

we see the mouths moving
in utter silence, but of
course we know exactly

what the mouths are saying.

"This Is Thursday. Your Exam Was Tuesday."

It is a fine, beautiful
and lovely time of warm dusk,
having perhaps just a touch
too much

enveloping damp;
but nice, with its idle strollers,
of whom I am one,
and it's true,
their capacity for good

is limitless, you can tell.
And then—ascending
over the roofs, the budded tips
of trees, in the twilight, very whole
and official,
its black
markings like a face

that has loomed in every city
I have known—it arrives,
the gigantic yellow warrant
for my arrest,
one sixth the size
of the world. I'm speaking
of the moon. I would not give
you a fistful of earth for
the entire moon, I might as well tell you.

For across the futile and empty
street, in the excruciating

gymnasium, they
are commencing—
degrees are being bestowed
on the deserving,
whereas I'm the incalculable

dullard in the teeshirt here.
Gentlemen of the moon:
I don't even have
my real shoes on. These are some reformed
hoodlum's shoes, from the Goodwill. Let

me rest, let me rest in the wake
of others' steady progress,
closing my eyes,
closing my heart,

shutting the door
in face after face
that has nourished me.

Falling

There is a part
of this poem where you must
say it with me, so
be ready, together we will make
it truthful, as there is gracefulness
even in the motioning of those
leafless trees, even in

such motion as descent. Fired,
I move downward through it all again
in an aquarium of debt, submerging
with the flowering electric
company, with March the 10th, 1971,
its darkness, justice and mercy

like clownfish, funnily striped.
Let them both as a matter of policy
redevour the light that
escapes them, Shakespeare
had just candles, lamps,

Milton had only the
dark, and what difference? as
poetry, like failure, is fathered
in any intensity of light, and light
in all thicknesses of darkness,

as your voice, you out there,
wakes now, please, to say
it with me: There
are descents more final, less graceful

than this plummeting
from employment; it is the middle of a false

thaw, the ice undercoating
of a bare branch is
in the midst of falling. Where
can it all be put except
in this poem, under us, breaking this fall,
itself falling
while breaking it? Look
at this line, stretching out, breaking even as it
falls to this next, like a suicide,
the weather singing
past his face, and arising to kill him
this first last line in weeks.

Students

They hold out their hands crushed
by misfortunes and I kiss
my fingers, touch my lips.

When they talk I can't help it,
I recede,
the words fall down and break.
I shut all the windows of my house
and look out onto the green lawn and am ashamed.

Students, for me, life
is just the ice-pick lying
beside the letter from the County Clerk
of Court, and the hesitation
of a hand between them,
hand I can't get
my own hand out of.
And the world—it's merely this place

of unfair vending machines
and women with short hair dyed red
who order another, and weep, and are unmasked.

Then later the world
is a repetitive street.
The hour is too late,
all, all is closed.
The red-haired woman touches the single
discolored tile in the bathroom.

She touches the marks the elastic

makes on her belly, her shoes awry.
She journeys
into the vast bed.
She reaches to the lamp
and makes it dark, relaxing.
She is not rising or even moving
but like many people at the verge of the dream
she feels as though she begins, now, to fly.

What This Window Opens On

Several of those faces on the avenue
are blossoming
into that light thrown always toward them
off the interminable, blue

backstretches
they gaze upon hopefully.
And from what separate, enraged oceans
can they possibly expect

to save themselves,
and for what? At times I say, obviously
this window opens
upon the seas and the blindnesses, it is from

this very window
that the signal will at last be issued for
the taking of our own lives.
Other times I suspect

that among the trembling inner organs
of a captured bird, people
are climbing into buses in the morning fog,
and I observe

a woman, how the movements of her parts
conspire to propel her
from grayness into grayness, vague
injustices attending her
steps until I wonder
what

can they possibly mean, down there,

by their arms and legs?—
until I wonder
what the voices must mean when they are singing.

Titles in the Carnegie Mellon University Press
Classic Contemporaries Series 1989-2017

Jon Anderson
In Sepia
Death & Friends

Peter Balakian
Sad Days of Light

Aliki Barnstone
Madly in Love

Marvin Bell
The Escape into You
Stars Which See, Stars Which Do
Not See

Catherine Bowman
1-800-Hot-Ribs

Michael Casey
Obscenities

Cyrus Cassells
The Mud Actor

Kelly Cherry
Lovers and Agnostics
Relativity

Andrei Codrescu
License to Carry a Gun

Peter Cooley
The Van Gogh Notebook

James Cummins
The Whole Truth

Deborah Digges
Vesper Sparrows

Stuart Dischell
Good Hope Road

Gregory Djanikian
Falling Deeply into America

Stephen Dobyns
Black Dog, Red Dog

Rita Dove
Museum
The Yellow House on the Corner

Norman Dubie
Alehouse Sonnets

Stephen Dunn
Full of Lust and Good Usage
Not Dancing

Stuart Dybek
Brass Knuckles

Cornelius Eady
Victims of the Latest Dance Craze
You Don't Miss Your Water
The Autobiography of a Jukebox

Peter Everwine
Collecting the Animals

Annie Finch
Eve

Maria Flook
Reckless Wedding

Charles Fort
Town Clock Burning

Tess Gallagher
Instructions to the Double

Brendan Galvin
Early Returns

Amy Gerstler
Bitter Angel

Patricia Hampl
Resort

James Harms
The Joy Addict

Terrance Hayes
Muscular Music

William Heyen
Depth of Field

Edward Hirsch
For the Sleepwalkers

Garrett Hongo
The River of Heaven

Richard Hugo
The Lady in Kicking Horse
Reservoir

Colette Inez
The Woman Who Loved Worms

Mark Jarman
The Rote Walker
Far and Away

Laura Jensen
Memory

Denis Johnson
The Incognito Lounge
The Man Among the Seals & Inner
Weather

Mary Karr
Abacus

X. J. Kennedy
Nude Descending a Staircase

Carolyn Kizer
The Ungrateful Garden

Peter Klappert
The Idiot Princess of the Last
Dynasty

Greg Kuzma
Good News

Dorianne Laux
Awake

Philip Levine
One for the Rose

Larry Levis
The Dollmaker's Ghost
The Afterlife

Thomas Lux
Sunday
Half Promised Land

Thomas Lynch
Skating with Heather Grace

Jack Matthews
An Almanac for Twilight

Mekeel McBride
Wind of the White Dresses

Irene McKinney
Six O'Clock Mine Report

Wesley McNair
The Faces of Americans in 1853

Joseph Millar
Overtime

David Mura
After We Lost Our Way

Carol Muske
Skylight

William Olsen
The Hand of God and a Few Bright Flowers

Dzvinia Orlowsky
A Handful of Bees

Gregory Orr
Burning the Empty Nests

Greg Pape
Black Branches

Joyce Peseroff
The Hardness Scale

Kevin Prufer
The Finger Bone

William Pitt Root
The Storm and Other Poems

Mary Ruefle
Cold Pluto
The Adamant

Ira Sadoff
Palm Reading in Winter

Jeannine Savard
Snow Water Cove

Tim Seibles
Body Moves

Gladys Schmitt
Sonnets for an Analyst

Dennis Schmitz
We Weep for Our Strangeness

Jane Shore
The Minute Hand
Eye Level

Dave Smith
The Fisherman's Whore
In the House of the Judge

Elizabeth Spires
Swan's Island

Kim Stafford
A Thousand Friends of Rain: New and Selected Poems 1976-1998

Maura Stanton
Snow on Snow
Cries of Swimmers

Gerald Stern
Lucky Life
Two Long Poems
The Red Coal

James Tate
The Oblivion Ha-Ha
Absences

Jean Valentine
Pilgrims

Ellen Bryant Voigt
The Forces of Plenty
The Lotus Flowers

James Welch
Riding the Earthboy 40

Evan Zimroth
Giselle Considers Her Future